HARBOUR

HARBOUR

Poems by

Miranda Pearson

OOLICHAN BOOKS

LANTZVILLE, BRITISH COLUMBIA, CANADA

2009

Library and Archives Canada Cataloguing in Publication

Pearson, Miranda

Harbour / Miranda Pearson. Poems.

ISBN 978-0-88982-261-0

I. Title.

PS8581.E388H37 2009   C811'.54   C2009-904761-6

We gratefully acknowledge the financial support of the Canada
Council for the Arts, the British Columbia Arts Council through
the BC Ministry of Tourism, Culture, and the Arts, and the
Government of Canada through the Book Publishing Industry
Development Program, for our publishing activities.

Cover photo: Christopher Grabowski

Published by
Oolichan Books
P.O. Box 10, Lantzville
British Columbia, Canada
V0R 2H0

Printed in Canada

For P.

CONTENTS

1
Touched

2
Preservation

3
Liminal

1
Touched

Doctor H.

Patient Jane states today
that she is not able to *do*
for her family as she ought, and,
in truth,
I see little prospect for improvement.

Has the patient been of sober habits?
Unfortunately
not.

She becomes excited by
heat of climate,
                    disappointment in love,
                    the change of life,
                    the death of her mother.

Jane uses very profane language.
She states she was taken to London and torn to pieces,
fancies the moon
is a man of blood.

The cause of her insanity is
almost certainly lactation—
she overly suckled her child.

Flighty.

Jane is herself
the daughter of a medical man and has received
a superior education, but she will not
occupy herself usefully—

cannot even be induced
to engage in needlework.

Today she supposed herself
The Queen and very beautiful.

When good tempered, Jane
chatters almost incessantly, but when cross, scolds
and makes herself as unpleasant
as she possibly can.

Now she fancies she is on fire,
and is in a tearing hurry. Now
she has conversations with The King,
awaits his commands.

Now she thinks she is a foreigner
and has forgotten English
(stops her ears, tufts of straw upon her shoulder).

We have tried Jane on brandy for medication,
she has become quite stout, cheerful and industrious.

She sings a good deal during the night
as well as through the day.

She takes her food quite well but
will sing at night, and will dance and sing
for half an hour at a time.

Now she spends most of her time writing
stuff she calls poetry
and rummaging over church matters.
Talks incoherently about being married.

Patient Jane observed in writing activity.
Discharged.
Uncured.

Jane

Whitechapel bells, please
ring for attention. Pray
remember the poor lunaticks and put
your charity into this box
with your own hande.

I have been here for
five years, you are my
famaly now. Even the
basket-man and the fire-cat,
even the keepers, yes,
even the Physick, Dokter Handwriting,
(Dokter Shakey, Dokter Red-Eyes...)

Nights,
I would embroider
in my bed, first by the light
of an oil lamp, and then
in total darkness.

Was it then
I went blind in one eye?
Began to draw on calico?

(The drawings belong not to me
but to the spirit world)

    Blood-
    letting, calamine and
    camphor. Sparrows, ivy,
    flowers.

Dokter Handwriting, am I
rekovered? Is it time now
to go down Featherbed Lane
and up Corkscrew Hill?

       (Sweetness coyed love
       into its smile).

England.
She hasn't a bloody leg to stand on.
Stands but on one foot.

       (Sparrows, ivy and flowers.
       Pasture of dying
       cowslips whispering
       outside the window.
       A floor-to-ceiling aviary
       filled with song-birds)

I'm stroppy. Distracted.
Discharged, whether cured or not.

Oh yes, I'm cured
(as ham is
kured).

Asylum

You go back and it's boarded up,
that elaborate brick building.
Signs: *Dangerous. Keep Out.*

The night of the hurricane twenty years ago, the end
of a decade working here
and you lay on the floor, the windows
rattling, wrenching from their hinges. In the morning
leaves drifted along the hospital corridors,
the driveway blocked with trees, fallen giants.

It was park land back then, sculpted and sloped,
a smoothed nap of lawn.
Intense sanity of the flowerbeds,
obedient rows of tulips, contained and responsive
to the gardener's hand.

Now these gardens are overgrown,
a buried civilization. Reaching arms
of thistle, bramble, rhododendron
(that dowager in purple).
Still, the old hospital—rising russet
from a gentle sea of bobbing cowslip—
is greater than the shadows and ghosts.

It always was frightening. Enclosed.
Mysteriously complicated.
There's the glass conservatory where the patients
used to sit, sucking tea from thick white china;
few of them ever qualified as a Plath or Ophelia,
or any other   mad heroine (their scarred temples).

Wax flowers under glass bell jars.
Engravings of Queen Victoria, Balmoral.
No panes left in the windows to that nursery world
with its strange rules,
where they thronged and wandered,
were kindly—and not so kindly—herded.

Nature has taken over. The red brick is barely visible
under the churning power of the grasses.
The local people—who used to be afraid of this place—
come here now to walk their dogs. Hush.
Let grass grow, thorn kindle
    and climb the walls.

Shift

Eight or twelve hours long
with an hour's break. In this way,
our time is divided, the watched clock
a segmented cake.

But it's different for Jane,
her neat trotting to and fro.
One of the hidden people,
shiftless, her time melts
over the thick iron radiators,
the afternoon a stretched-out yawn.

Jane marks her days
with a pocket-full of treasure,
her window sill an altar
crammed with hospital drift,
her fingers clenched tight over
some stalks of grass she
picked today, a ball of hair
from the bathroom, half a cigarette,
a flash of silver
from somebody's chocolate.

Winter (1)

It's winter and the radiators gurgle and scald.
The nurses are getting tired
of the low pay, the skivvy work,
the prospect of working over Christmas again,
changing diapers while the manager
reads *The Sun* and smokes in the office,
his size twelves up on the desk.

You buzz into the locked ward,
meet the wall of warm air, the eye-sting
of stale urine. Shrug into your white coat,
pull on the powdery second skin
of plastic gloves (keep a spare pair in yr. pocket),

lug sacks of wet and muddied laundry—these
are the facts of life. Sit in the dark
with a dying man as he hallucinates
crashing fighter planes, as he
shouts out to his co-pilot.

Tie bibs, spoon the soft food,
carefully wipe the shivering bird mouths.
Lift the white, onion-skinned hand
of a woman as she repeats her dead
sister's name. Do not yourself have a name.

The patients are drugged to a stupor
and the nurses also drink; a skyline of bottles
under the desk "for Christmas", dark rum and Bacardi—
sticky stuff, like medicine.

After the shift, meet the others
for a drink at the Staff Social, pint after pint of lager
till our faces rust and words slur.
Holding each other up, we weave
and skate along the sweeping driveway,
to the gates.

Four Found Poems

From *Broadmoor, a History of Criminal Lunacy and its Problems* by Ralph Partridge

1.

One is struck
by the gallant efforts
of both staff and patients
to gloss over the bleak facts
of the situation.

But provided an insane mother
has no more children,
she is unlikely
to feel a temptation
to repeat her crime.

2.

A high wall surrounds it
and no woman has escaped
in more than eighty years.

There is an exercise yard
where some of the
distracted women

have tamed wild birds
well enough to call them
by pet names

and feed them crumbs
out of their mouths.

3.

Occupational Therapy
begins with the laundry

and from there
they may move to the work room

or to the kitchen,
which is—

for some reason—
unpopular.

4.

Female vanity—
as much as female jealousy—

persists under
the sway of insanity.

The first sign
that a woman is emerging from shock

is when she
starts to comb her hair

and reach for lipstick.

Helen

Oh, so it's called depression (*thank* you Doctor)
and it would help if I could *talk* about it.
I see. Talking. A language
for other families, foreign to mine.
We spoke fluent silence, a rich dialogue all its own.

All very well to say,
choice, that's what life's all about,
when you're the one able
to wake up every morning
knowing which door you're going to walk through.

Easy for you, Doctor, with your silver Audi
and that fat dog of yours snoring under the desk,
your bare toes pigging its fur. I saw.
Easy for those Nurses too, sitting
in therapy's fairy circle naming *feelings.*

What about a want, a want of feeling?
What about the nagging and perpetual
with-ness of my flesh, my puffy quilted face?

No one would dream I was what I was.
I used to clean my kitchen floor
every morning when it was still dark.
Get down on my knees and scrub.
It was my way of knowing the world,
a touchstone. Here, I am another
rubberized old woman in her damp cellar.

And there are still, there will always be
the corridors. Curved like empty trains,
miles of green floor
waiting to be polished.

Helen's Window

I watch the tree
singular
in the courtyard, its fallen figs
hard and forgotten
like the unchosen.

It is going to snow.
The fig tree outside my window has
grey leaves—prayer hands.
The ground dry, mute.

There is a bluntness
to the day, the air
flat, suspended.
You might use the word *frigid*. Or—

if you were another sort of person—
you might say,
        how elegant,
the tree's bowed head, its
folded hands.

Listen. The sky
is beginning to speak.

Winter (2)

The days are dark and short,
a mustard-yellow sky crouches over the hospital.
Bash out "Jingle Bells" on the piano, my foot
stamping up and down on the pedals.

The giant flat-screen TV booms suggestions
for the perfect gift, we wear holly earrings
with our white coats, eat the Black Magic
that relatives bring.

The patient's needs are always the same:
to be maneuvered out of bed, deft removal
of the yeasty, sodden pad and (*mind yer back*)
heave him onto a commode.

Washcloth at the body's fulcrums,
the soft neck, the gummy newborns' eyes.
Arms are fed into sleeves, feet into socks.

Fresh diaper. Our hands
braided together under the body and
one two three   into the wheelchair.

Dinner: We spoon dribbles of
puréed turkey, puréed carrots
into slack mouths.
Blue and pink paper hats
perch on silent white heads.

They sit, curled like commas.
Serious porcelain profiles.
    A few flakes of snow wander
                                    outside the window.

Josephine's Window

The moon's a peach,
low on the land. Steady

and so round, rounder than anything
we could clutter our way with.

There go the geese,
their looped italics across

sky's spilt ink.
I want to lick it.

Soon the moon will change
into a handsome white tux,

uninvited guest at the dance,
patrolling my window.

Stalker, stranger,
par excellénce.

Electric

My first time, I was impressed
by the team work, the purposeful tension
in the doctors and nurses as we
hovered over the body
with the serenity of goldsmiths
hammering over a bench, knowing
our instruments, knowing our hands.

Stand back!
A type of magic, ashes to gold
with a flick of a switch.

I wanted smoke and top hats, doves
to force themselves free
from between his clenched teeth.
I wanted him to open his eyes and smile,
really smile, get up and shake himself,
walk out of this hospital, a happy man.

He was unconscious. He would not remember
the white coats gliding over him, turning him.
The laying on of our silvery, plastic hands.

I thought about his mind, his education,
why he would hand it over so easily
because a doctor told him to.

      Stand back.
      Can it really be true?
      The doctors say it is true.
      And that is all they say.

Black-Out

Last night at the pub after work, river of crowds
a happy tirade, ear-splitting table of nurses, women
let loose average size 16, shawls, Liz's matronly bosom
and Dickensian long hair flung as she laughs then
the lights jitter, flicker, go dead and we
stagger about in the black, gather in small groups
calling out each other's names getting a bit scared
till they light candles and a few of the girls
start playing pool by candlelight and Liz says let's sing
her sweet voice rising up:

>   *Iowa, Iowa, Iowa City,*
>   *when you're in love*
>   *you're so clever and witty,*

then I start *Don't Be Cruel*—
it had been playing in my head all day.

Josephine

She closes her eyes and it's
1942. She is the débutante
in the hand-tinted photograph
wearing the long green dress, satin gloves,
pearls at her throat.
Her young fiancée in his uniform
admires her song as it fills
all the corners of the room, and Josephine
is careful to turn her shoes out
as mother taught. Josephine sings
of how once a nightingale sang
in Barclay Square. The other patients
sit around the thumping piano.
A drowsy semi-circle on plastic chairs,
they hold tambourines, triangles, drums.
Some sleep. But Josephine sings,
eyes closed, head tilted back,
a pulse at her neck flickering, hands
clasped at her heart as if holding
a small bird, a sparrow, say, or a wren.

Good Morning Edith, Tea or Coffee?

Blood is leaking out of the cracks in my cranium.
What should I do?
Change rooms? Move out?
I've had a housing problem all my life,
but you have to be flexible—though not too flexible
or you turn into a pretzel, and now I'm a snapping turtle.

I can't complain.
Anything that smacks of the slightest criticism
and they throw you into a ditch or
into a mental hospital where they o.d. you
on abusive substances and give you hard labour.

They line you up and assess you,
but they couldn't assess themselves
out of a wet paper bag.
They expect you to live with men who smoke
forty-eight cartons of cigarettes in less than a month
and are still strong enough to kick down a wall.

With all those vast battalions of staff
you'd think they'd find the time but oh no
flip-flop into their dirty games, you can see it
with your naked eye, pay-as-you-can tragedies.

The more I work the slimmer I get
because of all my invisible maladies.
I'm not one of those social butterflies
hopping all over the planet,
singing and dancing and having dinner,
then trying to catch up with an education in an erudite age.

Every decision has a minimum of seventy ramifications,
that is why I cannot believe in love.
The people on the street, what marketable skills do they have?
Only violence.
Personally, I can't even lift a two-litre saucepan.
That is why I refuse to reproduce.

          Tea, please.

Newborn

Shocked and numb, the new mother staggers to the bathroom. She is herself newborn—into a distressed and bewildered cow. What happened? Her bulk levers itself through the dark room, she gropes for the window ledge, grasps the back of a chair, her big legs tremble. Somewhere she is aware of appearing ridiculous, hospital nightie gapes, her buttocks exposed, white.

The nurse's shoes squeak. *This way*, she guides, in her slim uniform, her cardigan sweet with baby powder. The big woman—the *new mother*—knows her own body reeks of pungent tinny blood, sweat. That her hand on the nurse's arm is gripping too hard. In the neon-lit cubicle she uses the bars to lower herself stiffly down, starts to weep as the pee stings.

This is what it will be like to be old and truly helpless, to need a girl like you to help me limp through a room and sit on a toilet, to be lifted up like a frond of seaweed by my own life.

Prisoners

Through the
long

dark
bars of the crib

the mother
and the baby

observe
each other

Break

Winter sun, tang of citrus oil at the lunch-time yoga class,
this one quiet hour
when the hospital workers stretch and breathe.

(Warrior two, warrior three. Gaze
on the middle finger, hold

for five breaths).
I know one thing: God loves me, and forgives.
My gods are trees and animals, they do not know blame

(downward dog, upward dog,
crow, cobra).

The teacher's voice tells us to go to
a quiet place deep within.
I lay my palms across my belly.
Twinned hands

imagine a spiral, a mandala (the lost children).
Over the loud speaker:

> *Code Blue*
> *Code Blue*

Detox. Notes

non-ambulant female/
escorted by police/
unable to care for self/
verbally threatening.

staggered gait/
alcohol noted on breath/
slurred speech/

verbally abusive towards staff/
no apparent injuries/

superficial abrasions to face left side/
abusive and threatening/
escorted to holding room three/
abusive to writer/

too drunk/
unable to sign/

money: none/
I.D.: none/
nearest relative or friend: none/
sex: female/
dependent/
codependent/
employed/
homemaker/
student/
none of the above/

abusive to writer/
physically threatening
no apparent injuries/
sleeping prone position/
respirations: regular/
no distress noted/

sleeping supine position/
respiration's regular/
no distress noted/
appears asleep/

appears awake/
sitting on mat/
standing in holding room/
banging on walls/
verbally abusive to writer/

requesting discharge/
able to care for self/

valuables returned/
own arrangements made/
programme complete/
entered in research box #2/
attendance at self-help group recommended/

do not write below this line.

Jane's Window

What is the name of that bird up there
against the cloud? The shape
of my two hands,
fanned out
heart?

Edith's Window

Pots on the sill
may deliver shoots
frail as lime-green rain

       I fold seeds
into the dark
sleeve of earth

envelope
for these letters
            sent

New Year's Eve

The year before—the one
when I was sick with it—
I sat on the neighbour's sofa,
gingerly. Everything hurt. I remember

rubbing the wooden armrest
back and forth, intent on the thing.
Around me, plastic cups, balloons, streamers.
Children, huge, sweating, almost teens now.

God help me, I was a downer at that party,
rocking there, examining the armrest
and sipping my way slow
through the drink like it was medicine.

I think I'd started on the pills by then
but they hadn't kicked in yet.
It was the waiting time. A dark room,
shouts of *cheers*, corks popping.
Pink insisting we *get this party started*
and my heart sick of itself
for running out of love.

I'm not wanting pity. This may
or may not be real. The "I"
or "self", only a vehicle
to move things along.

Say Whatever Comes to Mind

Clam-like, I huddle on the brown leather
skin of his couch. Unraveling my legs
on the thoughtful Indian throw, this room
might be the safest place I know
though I'm tight-lipped, mute
for his expensive minutes.

Let's say I *could* find the words,
pull them easily from my mouth
like party doves or whole, smooth stones.
Or, I might climb, ugly and weeping
onto his lap: *keep me, keep me.*

Forgive the roaring in my ears.
Let me lie here, inhibited.
Like the time I swam across the lake for bravado
then shivered for hours in bed,
unable to recover.

Portrait

Winter mornings, the sky still plum-tinted, I see him
through his office window, sitting by the lamp
as if he's been there all night, silhouetted
like the mother in *Psycho*, and I know

the Inuit sculpture is there, the family of plants, the
blue shred of fish circling in its bowl, another witness
to all those dreams. He'd say I'm a voyeuristic child
spying at the parent's window, but what's it like

to *listen* this early, careful interpretations
already floating across the room like tottering paper boats?
Do his own dreams interlace with his patients',
how does he keep it all separate

and doesn't he ever tire of that painting,
the one of the man, head in his hands like Rodin's thinker,
huge hallucinogenic flowers
bursting garish, all around him?

Spilt

Mid-sentence, I reach
for my paper coffee cup
and tip it, a shameful brown pond
sprawling like the Dark Continent
across his tidy polished floor.

As we now understand,
there are no accidents. Afterwards,
I think of amniotic fluid,
that moment of loss and gush, when choice
is done with, and the body spills.

It is so difficult to spill. To let another
spill into you. Graft onto your side
like a spliced rose. I sleep alone now,
plugged and blind-
folded, in hermetic quarantine.

I hold a widow's shawl around myself
and lie on this brown leather couch
as the years tip over, and I
talk about it, and talk about it.
Unraveling, growing older,
I talk about it.

Counterbalance

I remember the red stairs,
the office with its creaking floor.
The couch, the velvet throw, the tasseled pillow.
His desk arranged with artifacts—
pens, stones, a model ship.

Twice a week I lay on that leather couch
and when I could, recounted my dreams—
too often clouded by sleeping pills and wine.
For those years, no poem spoke.

I watched the brick-coloured heart
that hung from a crane in the construction site outside.
It slowly lowered and raised, raised and lowered,
a new building gradually emerging.

2
Preservation

Specimens

In the streaming silks of his placenta
a fox feotus floats in its jar.
Curled in a drawer,
racks of tiny skeletons
labeled "vole", "mouse", "lark"
lacey claw and spine, pink-tinged
beak and jaw; brittle rib's embrace.
In other caskets: pickled sloth,
cat, otter, snake, their sickled and
serrated forms cocoon in glass urns;
ivory and marbled, offal canned in brine.

Naked anatomy displays itself.
Wreathed in rotted garments
of champagne-hued tatters and
crimped shell; sealed
in mahogany and glass
the fabulous and the brief,
yellowing, fastened with thin silver pins,
formaldehyde's pervasive stink
and the ink of their Latin nomenclature.

Darwin's Path (Down House, Kent)

I walk his Thinking Path, hoping
its narrow and stony way can help shake
this petulant longing, this pointless
grind-on of desire
caught on my clothes, burr-like.

A charm of finch lift from the hedge,
refrain of *no, no, no...*

My old father waits in the car.
Once, he tried to teach me about the stars:
Listen, this is important,
some day it might save you—

Green gardens, thin rain,
Kentish mud on my boots.
In church this morning I helped my mother
dress the pulpit with spring flowers,
a rough wreath of yellow, green.
We carefully pierced stems
to thread them with wire.

How do you worship without belief?
After The Voyage, Darwin hardly left Down,
fretted about his health.
There was a daughter who never married,
preferring to stay and care for her father—
another form of cloister.

The view from here of the bone-white house
shows its classical proportions,
a Victorian doll's house.
Beyond the wall,
open countryside.

What can I learn from a man
obsessed with barnacles and earthworms?
He tore pages from his leather-bound books
so he could read more easily while he walked,
                        (see the white leaves
                        flutter out behind him).

In the tangled brown hedgerow,
the panic of thumping wing-beat,
pheasant's alarm.
Crows scatter raucous
and the naked oak   entwined with its glossy ivy.

Thin rain. I want to keep walking,
keep thinking,
                        but my father waits in the car.

Eternal Youth

What's your secret? she asks. It's after the book launch,
a group of us in a smoky restaurant called The Grizzly
House, spearing chunks of various wild meats and siz-
zling them over a rock too hot to touch; we are Nean-
derthals huddled together by a small fire at the mouth
of our lair. *Hedonism,* I reply easily, piercing a scarlet
wedge of caribou and flipping it onto the rock that
seethes now with garlic butter. Then again, maybe it's
just genes, moisturizer, nothing fancy. Keeping active,
avoiding dessert—you know, in moderation. Mod-
eration, we chew on that for a while. Then, growing
more reflective, I talk about being the youngest, how
I've always felt the left-behind five-year-old—despite
that being clearly so inaccurate now (laughter). But it's
more than that. How do you grow up when you're al-
ways walking beside yourself? A double, holding your
own hand, your own favourite child. I look round the
candlelit table at the poets' smooth glowing faces as
happily we spear and roast venison, bison, buffalo and
elk, our shadows looming large and patient on the
wall, their hovering attention.

Flight/Home

Two hours in and my head is still full of Canada,
my eyes red and blind with the

dazzling indifference of snow,
of mountain. Despite myself I have come to love

that hard place, come to make something
of being blown so far off-course. People settle

into a collective darkness,
a sighing reluctance to tolerate and a having to

(below, the showing edge of land,
impossible snow   celestial copper flush

                              of cloud).

                    ⤳

If it's true we each have a parallel life
where is she and what is her name? Is she down there

on a white northern plain? Or,
in England, standing in a summer garden

looking up at a jet stream, flexing her back
before she attends again to the earth, to her plot?

And we, in this stinking flying ship
(*I'm on a plain, I can't complain*)

in heaven's face, up close and rude
yet sealed off, so stuck

in our mortality, our blood-clots,
head-phones replaying some dumb myth

you will learn
and your classroom is the dark

belly of an airplane as it forces its way up
and over this gentle planet   blue and green

its cargo of weary humans who can't decide
where to spin out their lives.

※

Critical and irritated, you don't know why
it's turned out this way

though it's no more absurd than anyone else's story—
even hers, the one you say you envy,

that woman down there among the flowers
rubbing the ache in her back.

Because there's no place (like home)
there's no place, and you, yes you

chose this ludicrous back and forth, so
brutal and unnatural, you chose this

ripping yourself away again and again
as if to punish someone or perhaps

just to see what might happen
if you took the flying leap. Just to see.

English Dreams

Your daughter has plum jam on her hands,
all spillage and stickiness. Full of desire

you kiss me right in front of her
(she being there adds erotically to my role).

The dream is steeped in recycled cruelty,
my matchstick-girl sense of being grateful

to be at the table (what if I turned ugly?
Or angry? Chances rapidly evaporate

there'll be a chair at all)

≈

The usual pearl-grey sky.
Mother's skin itching. I'm responsible.

They went on holiday, black-and-white photos
of the family, Scotland, July 1962. Where was I?

Other recent archaeological discoveries:
Mum was ill soon after I was born,

she suspected someone was
poisoning her.

Your trouble is,
You're far too sensitive

True, true. But try changing
this late in the game. And anyway

permeable is not the same thing as
considerate. No, not the same at all.

≈

Embalment. In the dim light
of the Egyptian Room at the British Museum

mummified bodies lie like anorectics',
curled together in their stone nest,

so intelligent
they starved themselves to death.

Dad says the only intelligence that matters
is mathematical, proof of this theory

being the elite math schools
established secretly in Stalin's Russia.

≈

Another doctor told me you had stomach cancer.
Sad news—though at least

it's finally alright to touch you
now that you're nearly dead.

But wait, why didn't you tell me yourself?
And why try and cover it up?

My wedding. No bouquet.
I go to a nearby flower cart and ask for one

but it's small and limp, with no ribbon,
I'm furious, I demand large purple tulips!

Is my rage valid, or just another weak attempt
to justify my leaving?

(the rich trees around the house,
oak leaves glossy with rain)

I emerge through a small vent
into a Russian square. Statues are toppling,

a ballerina twirls on an elephant's back,
broken Buddhas float down a river.

Brother, sister, we have to run to catch the train.
I wish we hadn't hidden in the dark so long,

I wish we had more time.

Squash

The brightly lit cell, its windowless
cream-coloured walls brindled as they are
with shoals of rat-grey dabs, quick
brush strokes, or some crazed prisoner's
marking off of his days.

The trance. The fierce chase of the black
full stop as it ricochets off walls, sings off tin.
That tense interface between delicacy and aggression,
and how—within clear rules, the court's constraint—
you go wild.

From up in the dim gallery
I used to watch my father play.
It seemed a man's game,
wouldn't have occurred to me to want to try.

Though I stared, fascinated,
at the plum-shaped bruises he
strolled around with afterwards.
Were these thrilling blue medals part of being a man?
Didn't they hurt?

Now I push open the heavy door, step in.
Aim a vengeful *thwack* to that ball, black
as the pupil of an eye.

Regan

Three women in our late thirties, we agree to go and see it again, see what happens. Popcorn buckets as shields, we laugh nervously, we're afraid we'll lose it, be horribly triggered, regress to blubbering thirteens, and stay that way. The space-age, ten-screen theatre is half a lifetime away from the Sevenoaks Odeon; its dusty red drapes and cigarette-burned velveteen seats. Jenny and I sneaking in to the matinee, our padded bras and coconut lip-gloss of adult impersonation.

I'm just going for the added footage, says one of us. Me, I'm curious to time-travel back to an old self, unformed, a girl ardent for the glamour of suffering. And in the darkness, the wrap-around stereo sound, I'm sitting there drenched in a feeling I can't name—though it's close to grief—memory knocking, but unable to surface. There's Regan, cherubic and fresh, as we all were. And her mother, the self-involved actress, newly divorced but *totally functioning.* Life goes on. Though you might say, *Mummy's in denial.* Now I might say these things. But back then I was pure response, pure antennae. Who even noticed that Daddy was missing from the story? Who among us understood any of it, as we searched our inscrutable mirrors?

Though we knew some things—even if we couldn't have named them—we knew there was glorious justice in Regan pissing on the carpet at mummy's party in front of all her friends. We knew there was a voluptuousness in her tantrums. For we who could not, Regan spat and roared and threw furniture. Regan was mannish, foul-mouthed. Regan had appalling skin and didn't care; Regan had eyes like green traffic lights. She was the monster upstairs, she was the boss.

While our bodies were forgetting their childhood's lithe acrobatics, she crab-walked and spun, knew the erotic secrets of levitation. And Regan cried and cried. The long, deep, soul-weeping of the infants we could never, ever be again. Who were those men in black cloth skulking outside her bedroom door? Leaning over her, trying to hold her down? Regan snapped their necks, hurled them out the window. Regan daubed her thighs with bright, new blood, carved *help me* into her maggot-white body. Vomited primal, bulimic fury for herself, for her mother, for *us,* as we held our breath, teetered, soft, on future's curb. And the father? He *is* absent, is dead and gone, whatever the doctors and priests might say. The girl has been seriously misled and she is right to rage.

At the movie's end, we, like Regan, are recovered, calm. The lights go up and we are free to drive away in a hushed, expensive car. Bathed in relief that it is possible now to *de-construct,* to *comment,* to *discuss.* We have earned the protection of language. And that's another film entirely, where the quick hand reaches up from the grave—snatches you back.

Cynthia

1979: a bar spilling out
on to a London pavement. Summer.
Stockbrokers and journalists, ties loose, top buttons open.
You were there, amongst the men, your long legs
restless, kicking off confinement. You were too big,
too muscular for your flowered skirt.
Who were you kidding, Cynthia, wearing an Alice band?

I thought I'd always have you in my life. As if
old friends are pieces of jewelry
you can keep in a box. I thought we'd meet
every few years, somewhere hot if we were lucky,
lounge on a porch together
wearing Jackie O sunglasses, tossing each other
exaggerated thumb-nail sketches
of our lives, gossip-spiked, lavish praise, absolution.

Sundry children. Divorce, probably.
You would gain weight and be furious,
with your expensive American teeth,
your polished black hair, your booming voice
that spoke seven languages and was sarcastic in all of them.

Nights, you dragged me down Shaftsbury Avenue
on the hunt for authentic kebabs, impressing me,
sweet-talking and terrifying the waiters in rattling Arabic,
or Hebrew, or Italian. All those free drinks.

Beirut burning in *Circle of Deceit*.
You, doubled-up, sobbing in the empty cinema,
my bewildered, inadequate comfort.

I wanted only your bravado. We were feasting partners.
You'd phone late, knowing I'd always be up
for a spin out to Brixton or Hackney
in search of the real thing.
Walking everywhere, arm-in-arm like lovers
along the dirty pavements.

It was always summer, the windows open.
Islington, stars, the sweet smell of marijuana
under a magnolia tree, its generous perfume.
Later, sharing a bed, your stoned hands,
the startling adventure of unfamiliar skin.
Holding your wrist in the gesture of *no*.
Next morning the usual smoochy hugs good-bye,
the corrupt, loose loyalty, the complete forgiveness
of then.

Marriage to a Texan. The safe bet we'd always laughed at,
nicknamed *Pillsbury*. And it was Houston for five years—
post-cards of oil refineries, your sweeping
oversized handwriting demanding to know
what the hell you were doing there,
question mark, exclamation mark.
Cynthia, I couldn't have told you.
I'm the last person to give advice on marriage.

You appeared in London for snatched weeks,
gulping the summer exhibitions, films,
anything spicy you could eat with your hands.
At a party, sitting together on the stairs,
people threading around us, I lifted my wine glass to you
and you tumbled into me, again the sudden, violent weeping
and the inability to explain.

But then—somehow—you maneuvered Pillsbury to Paris
and I was the envious one. Mean, rude Paris, with its
sullen glamour, its lavender sky. Visiting, I listened,
confused, as you bantered conspicuously with the Maitre'd
at the Algerian restaurant. We stood on cobblestones,
watched a wedding procession and ate dripping patisserie.

Walked by the river. Breathed the rare stillness
of the cathedral, smell of polished wood. We lit candles
at the shrine of the Black Madonna for the baby
curled within you like a bomb.
Children caged you. Long before you'd
walked far enough, eaten enough, explored enough cities,
dared to glimpse back at your life.

Your appetite was too big, you were too selfish
to be harnessed by the small, steel tethers of a child.
Cynthia, I speak only as another selfish woman.
Childless, you could have become sleeker, funnier,
traveled everywhere, made cutting remarks
on how boring the rest of us had become,
been the favourite, wicked-est godmother.
But if one child moored you, two ran you ashore.
Something monstrous from your past rearing up.

The last time we met you were pregnant again.
Walking angry miles, ignoring the pregnancy. Still burning.
I fell behind with your crying three-year-old
while you strode ahead through the Tuilleries Gardens,
your black coat flapping open.
I wish I'd known more then; I had no idea
that becoming a mother can collapse a woman.

You walked me to the Metro,
we ate crêpes together in the rain, sugar melting
down our wrists. But I had got on your nerves this time.
Flippant, between lovers, childless, free.

～

Two years later, the phone call.
The stammering, a shaking hand over my mouth.
This was the past crashing in, breaking and entering.
This was photographs of us with long hair,
all hip-jutting pose, grinning into the sun.

Two days of flipping through my address book
for numbers I hadn't called in years,
the long-distance map lit up, the spread-out
of sparkling threads.

You had jumped. Plunged into the Paris afternoon,
into the sound of traffic.
Faces below upturned *(petals on a wet, black bough)*
a large body rushing through the air, flowered skirt
billowing up. The crowd gathering
before the police arrived, then moving on
to go about their lives, perhaps
hurrying through the street market
for baguette and tomatoes, or straight home
for a glass of red wine,
and a good nasty story to tell over dinner.

I think of the dent in the pavement. Is it still there?
Was it repaired? Who repaired it?
Did you drive out to the suburbs and do it there? Or
—more likely—you leapt—a huge, desperate bird—

from a grey house in the heart of that violent city,
with its dainty balconies and shutters closed
to the lives within, the swollen sky
lavender, before (or after), rain.

Dunblane

And today the children being chased—
not by each other in game—
but by *a real man,* his fat hands
bursting with guns.

Danger. Unbelievable
in black earmuffs and black
hat, eyes black as he
turns on them,
scuttling into corners.

What *is* this? This
small jagged island
with bombs in the litter baskets
and on the red buses,
the familiar shape of it's shores
licked by black oil?

I can only hear about it,
can only phone, invisible as spirit,
send love, support, blah blah

blah.
I am a deserter,
a bad mother.
Turning her back
on the delinquent child
and keeping the easy one.

Clipping a photograph
from the newspaper—
his pale skewed face
about to spit.

Brighton Beach

Crows take over the beach and fog makes me ghostly,
a thin visitor who floats like a child
believing she is invisible and in fact she does cease to be,
imagining her presence away into the white sky. Distant
squawking birds, the waves self-soothe,
a muttering release of themselves; they speak for me,
this terrible passivity. But what did I expect? Hard
shadows, passion? A man, charitable and generous
between children and dinner, charitable and generous
with no-name desire, its very declaration an act of dignity?
Smoke, wine, each other's mouths, alive—and yet,
and yet, if authenticity is to be alone, most nights
I would rather sleep with books than men. I will walk
and pick up beach glass, green, softened like some old hurt.
Choose stones to turn over, study the petty details
of dry-stripped bird bones, a diseased pear. Lie down fetal
on the shingle, taste its salt, its fishy damp. A brown animal—
ferret, rat? skitters by, mangy citizen of this place.
In the foggy distance: the West Pier, an exoskeleton
of rotting frame. Poetry, I've missed you, take me back.
Suck of sea on gravel, *break, break, break,* the past collapsed
in its delicate cage of bone, its hooped skirt and small black
   heart.

The Turn

When you finally return
from that misty place of birdsong,
greens and blues and
soft-dimmed light—

everything is strange.
Your long-neglected Vancouver garden
overflows with fronds, they are
jungle tongues, Jurassic.

And blooms, vulgar
peonies, scarlet-tropical, big,
bigger than the floppy silk rose
you bought on Oxford Street

to pin on your collar. Your body
can't let go, can't wrench itself around
to this bright new-ness.
A mill-wheel changing direction,

the water still pushing, still
churning, you cannot make the turn.
And the light! It burns
your pale blue eyes.

Kerrisdale

The real estate ad reads:
Elevate yourself to Kerrisdale.

See them
venturing down these clean streets,

the careful steps of the elderly,
their eyes, their blue

trembling hands.
Who knows

where they have been,
what they have seen?

Whole families erased, like tables
stripped of their settings.

They visit the coffee shops, the deli
for shavings of meat and cheese.

Turn shoes over for the price on the sole
(Away Melancholy, let it go).

And you, with your
hot raw heart. You too

wear widow's black,
scrape your hair back

off your white face,
your red-rimmed eyes.

Perhaps lipstick—
British Red.

#46

In Toronto I found your old house.
Walked wet streets, past
green railings and red brick, boarded-up
windows and looting squirrels. I crossed
the narrow footbridge, imagined you
cycling here, a child skidding in the rain.
You have always seemed distant,
a figure from my past or at a skyline way ahead—
or perhaps it's I who keeps you there.

The house is hung with wisteria; grey vines
drip down their pale promise, frost-bitten.
I used to say my heart was a well-made box.
Now it's more a waterlily—last time we met
I could barely look at you. Still, the blare
of bird-song, wind in the trees, restless as ocean.
You're thousands of miles away, living out
the choices you made. And I'm standing outside
an empty house, landlocked,
brown-edged petals eddying around my shoes.

The Royal Ontario Museum

Neanderthal Man is said to have a large brain
but what a tiny head,
a nub on a neck, in truth.
And today the museum is full
of enormous teenagers who look a lot like him,
thundering in packs past
Everyday Green Glassware of the First Century
and *Grotesque Head, Female.*

You can't go back and who would want to?
The smiling serpent skull and considerable teeth
of the Tyrannosaurus make one glad
to be well past those swampy times,
perfect though they were perhaps
                              for ferns.

There's a lovely jug, its shape a wasp's nest.
Another: *Lobed,* and this one: *Leech-Backed.*
Scraps of glass, green, blue,
full of light.

Millefiori: "a million flowers",
and *Mummified*—there's a word,
her withered paws, face aghast
at all that's happened.

A girl with a scarred burnt face
lags behind her group
to read the text by the Egyptian make-up display:

Beauty in Things Exist
in the Mind Which Contemplates Them.

I retreat to the European Style that makes sense—
and bores me. Flight: down a corridor back to Egypt,
on to the Etruscans, dusky frescoes
silently imploring like trapped ghosts.

Round a corner to
collide with Rex, his massive canoe
of ribs, his thick, whipping tail,

                                    those teeth—

Edmonton

1

All along the river valley: the flotsam of winter. Plastic bags bedraggle the slopes, swollen, blowing in the wind (American Beauty). The crackle of dead leaves, shocked, tinder-brown from the long grind when the city becomes a burrow and people, moles, so desperate for HMV Sound and The Gap they insert themselves down tubes and tunnels to (only) connect.

I'm in a hotel: part Disney, part chateau, part prison. Spires, battlements alongside the makeshift, the new royalty of Dairy Queens and Macdonalds.

2

This wide land. Distant mountains (slumbering arms, draped, maternal), arching sky. She wrote that she *moved here for the sky*. Skyscrapers, silver splinters beg the sky—though it's not listening—still, the buildings claw upward as best they can, streets—dry rivers flowing through concrete canyons, snarl of strip mall.

There was life here before, you know, says Marilyn. *You'd think there was nothing here—that it was only dead yellow land, dust and wind—before the railroad, before The Hotel Macdonald.*

There's china in a shop window, Queenie, her face so like my mother's I would get them mixed up. And Charles and Di, still together after all these years, smiling on dusty plates and hand-bells, in Edmonton.

3

Marilyn takes me to the peace that is the old train tracks, the inner-city allotments. We listen to the play and chime of leaves, their soft waltz. Two grey cats pour slowly from her doorway. She offers me a hand-kerchief, Belgian lace, the colour of prairie snow. Says, *I want you to have it.*

Walking back to the hotel along Whyte Avenue there's grit in my eyes and nose, my face screws up against the wind like a dog's. That night I dream I'm royal and am thrown and crushed under a horse as it jumps. The dream feels wild, hopeful, as if perhaps I am the horse and not the princess. Perhaps I am the accident.

Steak

Bison fold themselves under a tree, their huge spines
thick in a lovely range, their bemused gentleness.
And the zoo: its false concrete mountains and
bristling blonde grass, dust and glare—how would it be

to stay on, uncounted amongst the old
buildings of Winnipeg? The river is risen high,
higher than the city planners knew, and the people too
overflow their plastic seats at the food-mall.

Half your life left. Small clouds, birds flying by.
Not to lead a life by default (decay, pyre). Not to
raise my fork and puncture her skin, the massacred,
the cloven, fed on the puréed remains of each other

—it's a small thing, almost invisible.
One white woman with choice, the privilege of refusing
the body of a fawn-furred cow, her long brave neck, turned
into a glistening red package and the label that re-names her.

Artist's Model

She is facing the window, the fir trees, the snow,
waiting for the muffled thump as another clump loosens

and slips from the bough. Catatonic, a sort of
death state, the body suspended—her mind

wanders, spools out to that painting of a woman
in a twisted sitting pose, the shadowed mocha contours

of her back, in her raised hands a tambourine—
who was the artist? Not Bonnard, not Manet....

The melting snow seems risen, fat, an overhanging lip,
like fondant or dough. Idle *clop* as more collapses. A statue,

she can hear the clock creep, the student's
rasping charcoal as it searches out shape, form.

Who was that artist? Maybe Renoir....
The woman in the painting is holding an urn now,

tipping, pouring wine, a smooth
maroon stream of Classicism, if only

for the salons of the rich, for pleasure or consolation.
All bodies are beautiful and should be loved. She recalls

the teens at the lake, the one who, moved by the sacred water
pulled off his clothes and swam naked,

his friends hysterically clicking photos as he emerged
so they could post them on My Space.

So much is squandered. And the fallen urn too,
tumbling down stone steps, snow's soft

lob, boys throwing snow balls, broken....then,
paper rustles, quiet voices lift, begin to

flit like birds and she stirs, stretches, gathers up
her robe from its turquoise spill on the floor.

3
Liminal

The Architect's House

The car carves the West Vancouver shoreline
past hidden driveways, rhododendrons

to the glass house, half-
hanging from a cliff.

A scaffolding of trees surrounds it,
giant windows survey the ocean.

Grey Northern light. A creek
gushes between silver birch and under

a Japanese bridge. Sudden red azalea—
white butterfly for contrast—

a solitary fern
propped in a jar.

The creek clamours
down the evening, tongues of water

slipping over slick rocks,
quick, deliberate.

Love the body
and invent the rest. Summer-

skin tastes of flint and minerals,
like sucking on a river pebble.

We are all façade. Our hearts
concealed, remote,

but if we lie still enough,
breathe slowly—

we won't scare what may
linger outside—

a deer, or some other
gentle animal.

Tofino

You lie stomach-down on the sand
reading *The Kite Runner* and missing your son.
I can't reach you. Last night, insomnia again,

your unfamiliar breath as we journeyed
restless through the hours, both of us
trying to offload the past, the houses, the boat—

rich over-crowded paintings
with giant children in their foregrounds,
strangely bigger than anything else.

In Kabul, children shatter
as they ride the school bus. More bodies
airlifted from unimaginable ruin.

Here: paradise. Swimmers float
in the glassy waves, bob and dip.
I watch a man in black shades.

He could be you, with his brown
glistening arms, his dog nearby.
Techni-coloured summer, loud like drums,

the tight blue canvas of sky, blinding.
And the sea's big story, capable of joy,
the sudden kickback of an orca's tail, applause,

as if it were clearing the high jump.
And us too, our room last night
open to the sea

and thick with lotus oil perfume, it still
winds into my clothes, my hands, as we
lie side by side, quiet as saints.

Wet whips of kelp coiled on the sand,
its miles of rippled landscape.
Looks like Northern Quebec from the air, you say.

My friend's son drowned here.
We've agreed—no children, as if.
Though I thought it would never end,

that wayward tidal metronome.
At the inter tidal:
starfish, purple, and bulbous sea urchins

undulating mouths
yawn and clench, indiscriminate.
A heron waits, with its question-mark neck.

We can't say why we're here;
take what's available, the illusion
of intimacy or possibility of solace.

Put aside danger and the drama that gave our lives arc—
before we understood that arc
would appear, anyway.

Leaf-light on the trail. Miasma.
A deer's stately walk into the screen of trees.
Waves repeat and

repeat their messages as they do,
maybe yes, maybe no. Warnings—or nothing
but their own introspective song.

On The Beach

Under the sunshade the new family is huddled.
The baby twists on the woman's lap, living heat
of his monkey head against her thigh. She
arches over him like a crow while the father

turns away, stares at a book,
his back creased with disappointment—
none of this is what he wanted. Like a
cheap A-frame or a child's mobile,
can this triptych find balance?

What truce can they squeeze themselves into,
sweating and slick with sun cream?
The baby opens his pebble-grey eyes. Can he
fathom the arc of the new sky?

A jet stream splits the blue
like surgery. The woman's eyes follow
the thin white line; she has promised
she will never look back.

Father's Day

His head rests in the curve of her hip.
For a few seconds they breathe together.
She can see fir trees, the circling capes of eagles,
that strong Pacific surf—
his son playing in the sand.
It is Father's Day, their first day of real sun.
Soon he will look up at her, grin,
show his charming teeth and speak—
words she won't want to hear.
Then the boy will get sand in his eyes
and the father will jump up
and run to him. But for now
she feels his hair under her hand,
hears the ocean and the waves
of his breath. None of it
belongs to her.

Boys

In the glassy shallows: a small footprint.
Might be my son's: size five.
A boy about his age was wading here, left
his brief mark. I already miss him, my shy boy.
A mystery to me, his Aryan good looks,
his blue eyes so unlike mine.

Where did he fall from? He lists his hobbies
as electronic games and computer battles,
their jewel colours bright as stained glass.
Sometimes I feel devoured by cartoon monsters,
their cheerful jaws scooping everything;
though this summer we
grew apart a little, as if preparing
for the next decade
when he will grow taller than me,
a beautiful stranger.

Yesterday I met a woman, a painter, whose son
was killed at seventeen,
stabbed at a fairground in Vancouver.
I watched her stir her coffee, smile,
join in the conversation.
            Astonishing mothers.
Our hot anger and deep early kindness
toward the boys who step ashore into our hands,
then disappear, carrying jewels
dark within themselves.

Mother's Day

I dreamt last night that you were here
and I was holding you lightly at my hip,
the way I used to do. We were watching
a group of deer, grey and brown,
poised, alert, some pulling at the dry grass.

    The dream
      unfolded slowly, a rare gift.

Our arms outstretched we
traced the animal's leaf-shaped ears,
my fingers long, yours small, pink.

In the dream I kissed you,
rubbed my possessive mouth
on your cheek

and suddenly it wasn't soft
but had stubble, which is right,
you're fourteen now, your father
teaching you to shave. I woke then,
knowing it was right,

you're with your dad,
his wife, their baby. The family
you always wanted, demanded, from me.
The four of you will go for brunch
at Fuel, that cool new place in town.

I loved you fiercely in those
chaotic early years—friends said,
too much so. And, dear man,
I always will. Though it's quieter now,
more arm's length, more
slow-burning.

Smoke

She is going through one of those
phases again, she sits by an open window
smoking, the beautiful woman at the dinner party
who arrives alone, brings a wheel of brie, wears black.
She lets our little daughter paint her toenails silver
as her red mouth tells stories of
"yet another disastrous affair", and we laugh,
half envious, half grateful it's not us.
And for a moment everybody's buying it,
the long angle of her arm, her tinkling bracelets, tilt
of wine glass, smoke pluming out
into the November night, the moon's
slow-dance with her veils.

Island Through Rain

From here the island is mammalian,
smudged, crouching. Its low bulk like a whale,
or the bowed back of a man
resigned to his losses. There are islands
that will sink and disappear
as the sea rises up around them.
I have wanted to harbour you and
have you grateful, I send nothing
but thought. Vaporous threshold gifts
to carry you over—though you have
never asked for anything.

There are minefields
that have become bird sanctuaries
by simply being left alone.
The fixed island breathes
as if asleep in the rain and mist,
layered with its cloud ribbons, grey, white.
The currency of pale sea moving as it has to,
under sky's bleached silence.
You know there can be no rescue.
We grow calm, and the islands and seas between us,
calm, and older.

Coal Harbour

On the jagged rocks
below glittering condos,
        the heron waits,
hunched in his grey jacket.

It's always alone, head down.
Ignores the joggers and roller blades,
the white yachts with their
masts and nets,

"White Dove", "Magic Spell",
satiny flanks rising
and falling each day

while I wait   intent on the slow
wooing of the poem. How one word
        colours the next,

hand-over-hand, knots on a rope,
        slanting the light   reflections of boats
        quivering on the thin sea.

Lately, I have not looked up from the page
to see my life.

Cigarette

That weekend in Paris, the little sloping room
and the billboard across the street, remember?
The airbrushed photo of the giant model,
leggy and casual and always *there,*
touting her cigarette, her pouting, placid
gaze on us, sweating tourists lying
on the hotel's too-small bed, exhausted
by the day's glut of galleries, boulevards
of marble statues, their white, empty eyes.

Some men cannot walk a single step
without a woman to hold them.
Ten years back—your wife—the one before me—
how tired she looks, I thought,
her slow walk, her grey hair.
And you so boyish!
I thought other things too, things
I'm ashamed of now. *I* was the giant girl
outside the window then, waiting to clamber in
and lie with you. Not seeing
the new model already rising up behind me,
her long legs, her cigarette,
her sweet, concerned face.

Geese

An old love marries and you hear about it at a party
as you stand holding a glass of Pinot Gris
telling the contrite woman who told you,
really, it's fine,
patting her arm and in fact

you do feel something like relief,
this time it's finally ended.
Like the end of a board walk.
There you stand, try to be at peace about it.
After all, you didn't want him.

The boardwalk ends,
there's a bench, and a plaque:
"for ____, who loved this place."
They say the best way to forget
is to commemorate.

You sit and watch
a crowd of geese rise up

                        and as one, move on.

Thirty-Two Reasons for Flattening The Rockies

Because euphoria cannot be induced, it is a lucky breeze
blowing in from the Elysian Fields.

Because blue morning shadow drapes the slopes
the way a wave slides up a beach—

then recedes.

Because they're uppity, so damn full of themselves.

Because earthly conventions are the frame we
place ourselves within

and sometimes we must step outside,
even when that requires deception.

And the deception is recursive.

Because they love me,
they love me not.

Because it is Her Majesty's Pleasure.

Because we're only human and therefore compelled
to incorporate, engrave, graffiti, possess, plunder and eat—

especially if the object is sacred and beautiful.

Because Longinus was right but so, likely, was Freud—
and I happen to be a woman.

Because yesterday you said the heart was a waterlily
and Monet painted them again and again and again,

and always found more.

Because hoarding is a need
and I need

my mantelpiece to display
a collection of heart-shaped stones.

Because all homes are borrowed.

Because I am a glacier.

Because they hide the moon.

Because they're corporate,
just ask the Minister of Tourism.

Because of the sunken spines of tree roots,
surfacing like a buried line of poetry.

Because *birds build*   *but not I build.*

Because of the pine cone's scrupulous system.
Which might be a plot.

Because you sent me a poem with the opening line:
"Blue January light, cold, scoured, clear"—

Because *solitude* contains *soul,*
but winter is a tired metaphor for loss.

Because you can only love
when you're no longer afraid of death.

Because of the deer's stately walk.

Because bears and gods live up there,
and they're notoriously unpredictable.

Because the opposite of envy is probably admiration
but I'm not absolutely sure.

Because most of us, if we're honest, prefer a big sky.

Because they're there.

Postcards from Banff

You'll be glad to hear I'm writing again.
And you? It's Sunday, are you walking
in the bluebell haze of the woods in Kent,
in April? With the flint, the rain, the nettles,
the dock leaf nearby.
The grass will be flattened silver,
a furnace of wind loud
in the oak and beech.

Well, it's different here, but I know you'd love it—
these mountains are colossal corny postcard images
but real and not at all impassive.
The river way down there (toy-sized!)
a winding white thread of snow still,
where the glacier ate the rock.

I read about it—I know I was never
all that interested in natural history before
but some things seem more important than they used to.

I can hardly describe the sky, except as
"bright blue", the air so clean, a pine-sweetened wind.

Of course it's night where you are,
moonlight turning the lawn metallic.
You won't be out walking.
Probably sleeping with a pillow over your face,
the way you do.

I wish you were here.
There, I've said it. I wish you were here,
walking beside me, stopping for water at the turn in the trail
and taking in this view that even you
would have to admit, is spectacular.

We could be nerdy together,
wear shorts and hiking boots,
look up the real name of the furry mountain crocus,
which it turns out isn't a crocus at all
but the *Anemone Patens*,
usually found on south-facing slopes
late March to mid-May.

We could peer through binoculars
at that pretty yellow bird,
I think it might be the Western Tanager,
fairly common in this part of Canada—

okay, okay, I'll stop.
Distance makes a fool of me,
but today I thought of you, and how joy can be
as durable as sorrow, or as temporary.
But mostly, of how I wish you were here.

Climb

God gave men tongues that
they might hide their thoughts, but next time
let's be slower, let's be quieter.
A gaggle of chatty humans, with our
poles and backpacks,
our bad knees and breathlessness—we're up

where the gods live, and for a few hours
in our short, tortuous lives,
we can be alongside them. Jump the stream
as it pours itself loose, follow the trail,
the sunken spines of tree roots—

Where branched thoughts, new grown with pleasant pain,
Instead of pines shall murmur in the wind:
Far, far around shall those dark-clustered trees
Fledge the wild-ridged mountains steep by steep

—pause at wolf bane's bitter green,
Pine Marten scat, Old Man's Beard. Clamber crags
of pink quartzite spotted with their fine reefs
of silver lichen. Where lichen grows
the air is cleaner, quaffing it

both voluptuous and holy. The thin elated air
moves amid its own voices
and we want to be near, sun in our bones,
stand and gaze from the plateau

at the blue valley. Here we rest
and share food in our human way,
it is all we can do. We feast on this place,
this epicurean, open table.

Vegas

Girls girls girls
that will visit your room and be there
in twenty minutes or less
turn-down service
corporate blah blah
pick up your underwear
for your very own personal pleasure
stretch limo   amazing race
Paris under construction
400-count Egyptian cotton-clad
violin/piano concerto
girls girls girls
halogen-lit security
helicopters
for as little as $35
damn forgot my camera
phoned for one
swivel the plasma screen
to face the king-size
field of tulips

Vegas Fireworks

We startle   at the first crack
          red and gold spider-plants

blossom, dissolve
Christmas on our faces

a vulgar waterfall
glittering tentacles   spill

on the lakes' dark mirror
Vegas rain

everything is far away
acrid smoky ghosts fade

as another   gold fright-wig
          shrieks, boils over

          over and over
into this scarred night—

Roses 1

Once we were stripped down,
the tangled sheets a white calamity.
Now in a hushed conservatory
we sit across a starched tablecloth
elaborately reserved, the roses
between us a crimson fountain, a
poised geyser of reaching stems.
Voiceless, their courtly gesture is also
a quiver of gorgeous fists
obscuring the view,
the arrangement.

Corridor

split desire   supply   demand
      we vie with   confront   corrupt
      absent and unwritable

a dump of physical memory
      Puppet-bodies
stripped of all but the will to dance

and the body informs the dance   high-voltage
links to two   prompted by trembling

sprint
along corridors   door ajar   a pregnant maid
retching as she empties ashtrays

                        grip my wrist
this dog-like wish rocked into being
by the unique push

get a grip   fingers
print bruises   the body paused   petrified
donating the form

white earlobe
a petal
pinch   between finger and thumb
     an animal glimpsed
                  and gone

Trouble

I have tried to write a poem worthy
of the beauty and violence of opera,
of That Night. But when I think of it,
I'm stalled—
which may come as a relief,
as I know it was a concern of yours
that I would go ahead and publish
Embarrassing Details, the sort that
might cause Unnecessary Trouble.
Though I do have to say—
it troubled me immensely when you
slipped away at two in the morning,
the door closing like a book
leaving me sprawled in that
wrecked hotel room (that I paid for!
From my Canada Council Grant!
That wasn't exactly huge!*)
feeling like an idiot, mascara
muddying my cheeks and then
so hung over next morning
I could barely crawl round the Royal Academy.
But that's only one version.
There are others.

* Though very much appreciated and gratefully received

Petit Mort

She eases herself off him,
recovers last night's clothes

that drape various chairs,
the floor. Her red-

painted toes wiggle into high heels,
and—after briefly kissing him—

she slips away,
straightening her skirt. Later,

the cleaning staff find the body
and it's the usual grim scene

with the sirens, the stretcher, the
shrouded face

while high above the hotel: his spirit,
radiant and free, floats

up into the golden air of
another Californian morning.

Roses 2

Outlandish, a red burst
in February, a massive red tree,
they make a child of me,
their adornment, false and lovely.
Long-stemmed like rifles
each bloom in its prime, here,
today in this dining room
with its mirrors, and scallops,
and Bordeaux wine. Our
high courtesy as we clink
to beauty and not
to our wrecked lives. I have
always loved that about you—
the tipping point between elegance
and disarray, the way
you walk that line.

Time-Lapse Photo

He brings her tulips: vermilion
petals and serpentine ballet of stems.
Like a man
walking in the door
at the end of a long day

he deftly fixes drinks with the
doll-sized gin bottles from the mini bar.
No lemon.
No ice.

He cuts them each
a sliver of plum.

An impromptu home appears:
the low-lit, tousled bed,
books on the table,
tulips in a glass.

They plan dinner, check on children.
His hands—old lovers—
encircle her waist; that familiar gesture

in a room that could have been anywhere,
both of them comfortably at home—or
its reasonable facsimile.

Aperture

Fingertips trace
gentle pressure on a wrist's
pale furrow,
a rapid current there—runaway.

                Miles below, shining horror of white
which we must cherish, for it melts
and there are dark fissures, split seams—

In London the children
goofed about in the Tate Mod,
pretending to fall in the crack, or reaching across it

to touch fingers—the act of creation, that was fun.
Or, as the new wife of the French president
described their sex life: "upbeat".

Are happy people essentially unwise?
From up here you can view the world

from many different angles, and though
planes are heartbreakingly quick
and we ride on life's fragile momentum,

some beats can't cease,
                     despite the pause—

Day in the Life

I had expected fog but it was clear, warm
winter sun, sky off-white like a worn tee-shirt.
The doorman raised his cap and wished me "a blessed day".
Headlines read: "Boy admits yelling at tiger",
Obama was speaking later at Berkeley.
In Chinatown I tangled into a procession
of mourners, creeping black limos,
huge photo of the dead man's face
framed in paper flowers. There were
dried fish, parasols. Looped bridges of flags,
the silhouette of a trumpet. On the street
black kids swooped on skateboards
like sparkling krill. A homeless woman
crouched at the corner, her crying high pitched,
hard and shrill. Found a store called "Beauty",
but not the shade of lipstick I was looking for.
Lost myself in sunlight, up hills, down,
swung from clanging streetcars—transport of delight.
Another parade, winding river of placards:
"Women Deserve Better Than Abortion", carnival
of priests, children, smug smiling men
pushing strollers—I steered the other way,
took photos, it was all I could do. Kept seeing
a poster that read: "Winter Is The New Summer"
and though I knew the day was strangely amplified
and I a tourist, giddy, new in love,
I embraced it, held it close, deserved it.

Liminal

Old songs on the new iPod: *Miracles, Golden Years*—
  you are   lurched with sudden happiness

the plane tracing its way south
        along the coastline, lights glittering below,
                            this in-

between time, twilight or dawn—
nameless, at the margin, the

        pause of cloud
                lost in the body
of cloud, white fog   then flash

of green and blue, earth a glimpsed atlas
then gone

                your face at the window wet
and crying is perfect, we are
        soft, opened
up here
        in this liminal home, high above
the bridges and borders, real and

imagined, shadows and grids of an
                American city, who knows
if this is true or false   the trick

                    is not to want more

Acknowledgements:

Earlier versions of several of these poems have been published previously in the following magazines: *The Malahat Review, Contemporary Verse 2, Event, Studio,* and *Grain.* I am grateful to the editors.

Jane and *Doctor H.* were previously published as a chapbook "Jane", a Light Factory Production, in 2007. My thanks to Lois Klasson for her unerring dedication to the tradition and art form of the chapbook.

Jane and *Dr. H.* were written with the kind assistance of the curator of the Bethlam Royal Hospital Museum in Kent, England, home of the painting "Sketch of an idea for Crazy Jane" by Richard Dadd.

Four Found Poems are plundered from "Broadmoor, A History of Criminal Lunacy and its Problems" by Ralph Partridge. Greenwood Press, 1978

The quoted texts are from the following sources:

• *Away Melancholy,* Stevie Smith *(Kerrisdale)*
• *Ode To Psyche,* John Keats *(Climb)*
• *Beauty in Things Exist in the Mind Which Contemplates Them,* David Hume *(The Royal Ontario Museum)*
• *On a Plain,* Nivana, from "Nevermind" *(Flight/Home)*
• *In Honour of St. Alphonsus Rodriguez,* Gerard Manley Hopkins *(Thirty Three Reasons For Flattening The Rockies)*
• *In a Station at the Metro,* Ezra Pound *(Cynthia)*

Brighton Beach appeared on the Canadian Poet Laureate's "Poem of the Week" website. I am grateful to John Steffler for this opportunity.

My stay in May 2008 at the Banff Centre was essential to the completion of this book. I am grateful to all those individuals who make the Banff Writer's Studio the remarkable place that it is, and particular thanks go out to Don McKay, John Steffler and Mary Dalton for their skilled editorial input to many of these poems.

Thank you to Hiro Boga and Ron Smith at Oolichan Books for their love of poetry and the care they take.

Others I wish to thank for their support and encouragement in the writing of this collection: Barry Dempster, Betsy Warland, Eilis Carpentier, Mark Dombowsky, Dill Anstey, Andrew Currie, Adam Pearson-Currie, Mary-Ann Waterhouse, Rosemary Pearson, Michael Pearson, Jennifer Van Evra, Catherine Bush, Rick Sanderson, Isaac, Truck, Shelley Craig, Robyn Harding, Michael Dempsey, Peter Openshaw, and Price Montague.

I also want to offer my appreciation for the patients and staff I have had the privilege of working with—and learning from—during my years of working in Psychiatry.

Jane's Window is for Don Mckay
Cynthia is for Alan Friedman
Specimens is for Sarah Gull
Flight/Home is for David Pearson
Edmonton is for Marilyn Dumont
Eternal Youth is for Sally Cooper

Finally, my thanks to the Canada Council and the Arts Council of British Columbia for their financial assistance.

Author photo: Christopher Grabowski

Miranda Pearson is the author of two previous books of poetry, *Prime* and *The Aviary*. Her poems have also appeared in numerous anthologies and literary journals. A graduate of the University of British Columbia's MFA program, Miranda lives in Vancouver, where she works as a freelance editor, teaches poetry workshops at Simon Fraser University's Writing and Publishing program, and works in Community Mental Health Care.